GOOD LOOKING POMES

JOSEPH MATICK

First English Translastions

Copyright © 2026 Joseph Matick
Published Exclusively and Globally by Far West Press

All rights reserved. No part of this book may be reproduced in any form or by any electronic or mechanical means, including information storage and retrieval systems, without written permission from the publisher or author, except in the case of a reviewer, who may quote brief passages in a review. Scanning, uploading, and electronic distribution of this book or the facilitation of such without the permission of the publisher is prohibited. Your support of the author's rights is appreciated.

This is a work of fiction. All names, characters, businesses, places, events, and incidents are either the products of the author's imagination or used in a fictitious manner. Any resemblance to actual persons, living or dead, or actual events is purely coincidental.

www.farwestpress.com

First Edition

ISBN 979-8-9943356-0-4

Printed in the United States of America

Joseph Matick is the poet represented by Jack. This is the most recent and last found textual representation of his time as a permanently dissatisfied and chronic optimist. This work was widely regarded as the pre-eminent catalyst to his fixture as the foremost mind in aesthetics in literature, film and fashion. Though it was widely skepticized that it was the work of "Avec Jack" and its clairvoyant and influential subconscious and eternally hypnotic pedagogy that played into his fame, fortune and unpredictable sept-national status. Put plainly, this paved the way for self belief.

For:
Henry

Dedicated to:
Christian Dior
Thierry Hermès
Gabrielle Chanel
Yves Saint Laurent
Louis Vuitton
Valentino Garavani
Giorgio Armani
Gianni Versace
Miuccia Prada
and all the selfless champions of free speech,
who have so fearlessly devoted themselves
to the betterment of humankind,
ending fascism and every war.
And to other lies.

WINDOW POEM IN PARIS, FR

You can't see me, but I'm writing.

You can't place time
so you set clocks.

These are two sentences
placed perfectly atop
another.

Is another

until at once we all fall silently
as vertical dominos.

This is how you build a skyscraper.

This is how you tap a vision.

Through any medium you seek from
a certain future
you will certainly receive.

A phone is a medium
and the woman down the street
and the space we share the city with

and the city itself is large, captivating,
reveling in madness,

while I sit defiantly,
in silent confidence,
knowing the two of us
are one in the same.

JOSEPH MATICK

If a bird sits in a window

and another bird sits in another window
and they share a nest,

we could call them spatial creatures.
We could call them anything.

And yet we are birds.

We've only known flight.

We've only caught one another flying
every once in awhile.

It's exhausting to hear a city so loud,
and then it's not.

A response to the kitchen sinking
would be to fix a faucet

or build a boat.

JOSEPH MATICK

If you get called mad,
and it makes you angry—
you have lost the hilarity of the self.

If you get called mad,
and you laugh
the world will buy you dinner.

Somebody I love carried a flower
around the world today

and everybody smiled.

She gave it away.

She is free from watching a thing wilt
and eternally bound to a memory.

The memory is of everyone smiling.

JOSEPH MATICK

There's a garden somewhere,

where memories grow out of cow shit and mud.
You may be thinking about the words "cow shit"
instead of flowers.

It's my job as a professional bird
to remind you

the point will always be the flowers.
And that you and I are lucky enough
to see this from the same room—
you can see the stars, the moon,

and the madness we all blame the moon for.
I blame the moon for nothing.

And this is how you build
a new relationship to light.

JOSEPH MATICK

My response is as my response was

I am in agreement with the natural law
A little bit, for most of life

A little life for most the population, says the —
I keep losing myself for a reason

I keep loving myself for no reason

I keep reason away from love for every reason
for good

Some things will never reconcile and that is how
some things
show love

This is something else

That is a sure-fire way to lose a life, yet
Not yet, not yours

If you recall, we kept on running into bullseyes
And once or twice through fire

I have a specific intention to merge hemispheres
To leave no doubt

GOOD LOOKING POMES

To change your life and your life be changed

from my mere entering and you saying yes, because
We needed this, we needed each other

To be great and to be great to each other
And I was excellent in my life, I was on fire
You let me be

You let me become, before I became
something else

Ash, perfect ash

JOSEPH MATICK

POME

I'm a cracker, I'm a cow
I'm an American biscuit
I'm a cookie, I'm a crumb

GOOD LOOKING POMES

I'm William Blake wet dream
Cum stain, cum rag

Good swimmer, chicken dinner
First one to oblivion

I found the egg and laid myself
I came back for answers

JOSEPH MATICK

I came back to end the war you started all over me

GOOD LOOKING POMES

*

I get sick getting around

So I, the sit still linguistic juggernaut
Can find myself healthy and alone
And suddenly I realize, there's nothing
Nothing healthy about being alone

So I choose sickness and dealing with it all
All of thoughts in the entire world and their
Diametrically opposed motions

JOSEPH MATICK

I declare myself the humble and modest
I declare myself the best and most

I declare myself a custom, an exchange at the border
I see an Egyptian ring on an executioner

I salute and bow

"I never wanted to be here." she says

You're not.

And suddenly I'm on a train. And it's heading in one direction
And Me—having dealt with all the thought of the world and noise
Decide

I will play the drums and send my snares into the battery
And I Kick and scream

And I go to bed

JOSEPH MATICK

Just got out of bed
I'm thirty five, not yet
I'm looking for God

For the moment, So I can

Stop looking for anything, everyday forever

CONFIDENCE

Oh, how I've employed thee! To wear on my sleeves!

My sleeves, which are leather or leather looking and fall just above my rosy hip bones!

My bones, which are showing! And all exposed they are!

Through hereditary grace, of course. And not neglect or abuse!
Which all fall winter spring above boots which stand!

Withstand! Rain! And in all lambskin ole factory, old sheep and shine!
Spit! Shit! To platform my walk and position my stature!

JOSEPH MATICK

For runway employment! Or runway discernment!
My direction!
All discoure! In drig drag denim! Capitulating culture!

Spinning earth underneath me at increased momentous moment by moment by moment per hour!

Clothing! What have you to do with me?

May we run and never run out of style!

And forever compel the skinny martini spirits who dare take our silhouettes!

To chant our abstracted names! Which not an epitaph could carve as carelessly

as we in human drag, race toward visions

of Neal and eternity.

JOSEPH MATICK

RUMOURS

We tell them to ourselves, others, about others.

They come out of big mouths with tall cans drunk from small men.

At least that's what I heard.
If you press your ear to a seashell.
You can hear the universe sayin'

You simply can't
believe in anyone who claims to have any
idea

what to do with your life

The earth is about as flat as a perfect circle
Or the bullet that entered the president's head

Or the eyes that roll back when you say 911 was an inside job.
And that job don't work

And Paul Mccartney is dead

And all the people with sublime beauty in lofty circles eat pineal glands
It's all bullshit, Such bullshit

Nobody actually believes that we're all being watched.
But the people watching and the people being watched.
That's everyone.

JOSEPH MATICK

I want to believe in the world being a pure place...

I had no idea where this poem was going or where I was until I did.

Sally sells sea shells by the shore. Sally gives me 'bout a hundred million more.

Sally told me where to score. Cuts and sells you two for four.

I trust in Sally nevermore. I trust in Sally nevermore.

*

A stiff brimmed baseball cap covers just enough of your eye lids.
The hat reads the name of a team almost nobody can make out.

Your team isn't real. Your hat ain't even real. Your head ain't even real.

The things that live inside there are just waiting to die
or let you be supremely beautiful by believing in them,
giving them life and all of us.

JOSEPH MATICK

*

In New York, we're gonna sit like Humphrey Bogart
eating chesterfields and banging veins, starlets
smoking screens and headlights
pretending that life is beautiful and not full of noise

And marry the prettiest individuals and have all
these kids
and tell them all the shit we did

And he was just three or four years old
He didn't stand a chance and look at him now

JOSEPH MATICK

Anyway, life is beautiful, New York is beautiful
I don't love New York, but that place is beautiful.

GOOD LOOKING POMES

Who gives a shit? Ah, everyone when they're not
lifeless and adherent to lying.
I miss Alice Notley and wish she never passed from
this physical place.

Her voice is all I wanna hear sometimes.

And something about a dream

JOSEPH MATICK

and a perfect position and being too fucking bored
to not be too
flying high with ambition.

I believed in the almighty dollar.

And it worked—it really worked—because I
believed in myself
enough for others to. That's the game, kiddo.

But if you stop caring for money, and you will, you'll
be after something else.

And you'll get curious. You'll get curious, kiddo, and make up a wild hare to follow.

And the leader will look a whole lot like you but until then, it's me, your papa.

JOSEPH MATICK

ART

All over it, everywhere, laying in a canvas, spreading
my legs and frozen in time,
I was purchased for my beauty

Recognized in small doses over the course of a
lifetime
and in massive and exponential sums when I passed
away.
I gave my estate to my kids

Christie, Sotheby, Gagosian.

Even though they were incredibly critical. Their
noses
live forever. In the air, up here

If you wake up in the morning after morning after
morning after
Picard, Ricard, peinture, fracture, war, linguists

And televangelists can see the end
As is the case

If you are in the town floor in the back stall

With a neurological flair from perhaps over
medication, perhaps under
And optically speaking, there are green walls,
And orange pants and peoples, Paris, treasures

JOSEPH MATICK

Somewhere, if you are me, you are yesterday and you are here
But here is the bathroom of d'Orsay, backlot

Here is my living room night after night after night after scraped hands,
and no love, no wonder at latest hour,

13 or 23 or 11
Where's mom
Where's kiddo

Who's Beatles if this is the case
Art is everywhere

As is the case to be made, rather to make
And if this is it

May God know you in a corduroy jacket finding hard earned air
out of every inch of gripping, flesh and bone and tongue

JOSEPH MATICK

*

THE WORLD IS TIPTOEING—AMBLING,
CONFIDENT, AWKWARD, STEADY,
INCREDIBLY UNBALANCED, INCREDIBLY
PERFECT, THE WORLD

IS FULL OF TOURISTS AND MEMBERS OF
STAFF
THAT EXCHANGE PLACES FOR SEASONS

ONE SHIFT AT A TIME,

FOR SEASONS, DECADES, LIFETIMES AT A
TIME.

Joseph,

When I felt paralyzed, I wrote you this.

I don't know what it is that causes one to compulsively write.
I only know that there is a force.

I don't know who it is that compels one to write.
I only know there is no name.

If there were a name, us humans would have formed

a system of belief that would not incite war or rape the earth.
A system that would render my intent, my words useless.

But this—

This text is inexplicably vital and necessary.
I could not have written it alone.

I am almost certain that I did not.
What I am talking about is possession.

However, this word brings about a litany of images and associations.

I speak to the sleepless symbols that invoke you in your liminal dreams,
the spirits that awake too mischievously and immediately

to be believed in the waking world.

All these sleepless words; possession, intercession, invocation
have come to life within me.

And I will have you dictate and present this work.

—Jack

JOSEPH MATICK

October 30, 2024

98 Bd. Richard Lenoir, Paris
Joseph,

I knew. Something about these words would strike you.
That is the way memory works.

It works towards and against a present moment.

Dear reader, you and I are tasked with, privileged with...
directing that memory into a future.

One that is attractive enough for us to live
and strive for in the present moment.

It is the basis of what we call storytelling.

GOOD LOOKING POMES

It is, in essence, a way to keep us from infernal doom.

It is what keeps us from telling each other we know who we are.
Storytelling invites us into a dialogue about what words mean.
Though words will never finish their time with us.

And they will never leave us alone.

The structure of my world will be informed
by little glyphs and strokes.

It was the way I knew to write
when I knew how to write again.

I forgot that knowing again required forgetting.
Everything.

—Jack

JOSEPH MATICK

October 31, 2024

98 Bd. Richard Lenoir, Paris

I arrived in Paris. Something forced me into madness.
I sat down and wrote the best things I have written.

I knew this because I had no choice.

Belief is this kind-of superpower that people think they can have.
And they are right. As in, you are right to believe.

However, the world... as it stands is diametrically opposed to having.
We live in a world of disbelief.

Our world believes it can take belief, not make belief.
This is the reason that artists must exist.

The world doesn't know what to do with you and I.
It doesn't know what to make of us.

It doesn't know a world outside of handshakes and transactions.

The world must be used. It cannot be alright
with the further making of things,

GOOD LOOKING POMES

if it will never settle for first having been made.
For this reason, I stand to defy the world.

The non-believing world.
My son is 7 years old.

It is out of love for him that I condemn
all of society and its hapless creations.
I am out to terrify you with beauty.

I was once him, remembering...

I would like to be terrified with beauty.
I was.

I got older and learned of the world that takes, not makes,
I wanted to mimic those in power.

And so, I - became like you, an actor. A master of the craft.

I sought power to wreak havoc

on the terrifying beauty that I never elected for.
And I have reached the end.

Not of beauty, but of mastery... of the world.
I am simply here to make.

JOSEPH MATICK

*And I have made life, and new life and new pain
and I have surrendered.*

—Jack

GOOD LOOKING POMES

There is more beauty in pain than there is in beauty.

JOSEPH MATICK

I wish for you a greater world than the world does.

I wish for you a brighter future than history would suggest possible.
I wish for you the freedom of belief and of course, to know.

To know to never believe a single story you've inherited. Not first, without questioning it.
And questioning from curiosity,

Curiosity killed the cat. Lack brought it back. Jack brought a bat.

JOSEPH MATICK

I went to Paris because my son is here. My son is here because I allowed it. I work in the disobedience factory where French people flourish. I am unwilling.

And you are presented with the following.

JOSEPH MATICK

FLOWERS

I am traveling from France back to a place.
My country, my flag, my home, my heart.
Hey fire, how are you? You've burned out.
I used to complain about palm trees,
and confident nobodies. I used to become used to things.
Everything is unnerving,
and runs out east. I call an appeal to my heart,
which runs out east
like the rest of the west runs away.

Away from myself I run, and end up home.

Nobody wants to stay alive anymore
without running home. This place and that place—
I can say were once sterling.
I am not lost, I am home losing itself.
I am in love, loving myself.

I am at a loss with shrink-wrapped societies,
ideologies, identities, theft.
Who owns the West? Which beast, the East?
Why does the axis run across the X,
and who is the next X?
America—you will surely die
if you have ever lived.

Paris—you have mastered the art
of articulating dramatically the human experience.
You bore.

We need a new story,
if we need anything at all.
If we have anything to need,
we need first and foremost our brothers and sisters.
Where is my family? My son, where are you?

Whose am I? I love my country.
I kiss it goodbye,
and kick it out the nest.
It's just you and me now.
"I need nothing," my country says.
And it replies nothing, as I.

The only love I'll ever know is community.
The only person I'll ever be is someone who knows.
And what I know means nothing to you,
until you know nothing.
How can being empty feel so full?
Just ask the looking glass.

Looking for water.
There's none in its vessel, none in my blood.
I empty my china, break dams for the flood.
The end now is coming, the end now is here.
There's no beat to nik drumming,
no nik to beat here.

The West was never won. The war, never lost.
The East not another—tassels have been tossed.
We've graduated, gone. Diplomas are framed.
The office raided, the gunmen maimed.

I used to be famous—just don't know who, when.
I used to live alone,
with a million old friends.
I used to care deeply; still do, though, in fact.
This and that country, bedmates dear Jack.

I look to my neighbors, they give me the news:
the reds are all blues now,
the terms all confused.
The pimps have been punked, the pimped held a coup.
We couped the DeVille, see horns in rearview.

JOSEPH MATICK

(They're killing people out there.)
It's the subtext of it all.

GOOD LOOKING POMES

The context—we pretend life is beautiful
amidst this, and are right.
We are all court jesters
until you join the military or you use your tongue.

I like mine for kissing my lover—
or cursing the man.
I use mine while holding my love with two hands.
The other is you, in every instance.

I must admit, we are more just the same.
The only way in is to take back your name.
If you hate someone,
a small part of them is you.
If you love someone,
the whole you—exactly.
The only way out is through.
The only way in is you.

We walk through the portal on the 29th,
and in some small way change the world
in a massive way.

Don't fall for the discourse.
Fall in love. Find a hill to die on,
and a heart to maintain.
Every story is old.
A way through the winter heats up the cold.
A way out of summer—a ticket to there.

You could be me forever, for the price of the fare.

JOSEPH MATICK

I'd hate to be me, but I know who I am.
I am the other, the lion and lamb.
Give me a kebab, a shawarma,
some uncle named Sam.

A table for two, to play our best hands.
I'll be back in a moment, wearing his hat.
When the fat lady sings—she'll be skinny, in fact.
We've been hacked, we've been had.
We've been told to believe.
But believe in each other, get what you receive.

I'll come back from dinner with blood on my hands.
It's makeup, my darling—Hollywood somehow stands.
And stands to make a living, while I tap my thumbs,
flip nickels and nods to my neighborly bums.

Bum a smoke from a millionaire cop,
make him freeze, and a slow jaw drops.
Flip a Bic, drop a cherry,
drop my drawers and say peace,
and pray for a way to get out of the leash—
I mean lease. I mean what I say.
Even my mistakes slip my tongue the right way.
I've been right for too long.

JOSEPH MATICK

There's now nothing left—
but politics, policy, and property theft.
Countries we claim, flags that we fly.
And if you ain't living—find a reason to die.
Not a place, because it ain't here.
But if you convince me,
let's change things, my dear.

Put the gun down, that painting on the wall.
It's unfinished. 9th inning. Play ball.
Somehow it always comes down to this—
Home run. Crack a bat. Blow a kiss.

A big one, for my son and the world.
"Let's grab coffee,"
—Jack to Kate.

WILL YOU?

So many words
Come out
Out my mouth

And a couple of 'em
Will Be
Forever, It Takes

Three Words To
Say
"I Love You."

Two Words
To End
A Sentence
I Do.

I did a lifetime supply tonight
of bigtime shit, rockstar shit
perfectly

Met that chick
you wish you did and had a bunch of useless
thoughts

With all these infinity people
buying time for free
feeling like a million bucks

They were huffing this and that galaxy up their
entitled mouths and all us were
talking round religions and impositions
sexual improprieties, social securities
and trying not to blame their dads or exes and local
governments

On you for being you
Nobody would dream to do that

All these infinity kids

And you lost your mind so much until she finally
played the masterpiece
and very loud.

And together on time we forget what that was

JOSEPH MATICK

Being seen seemed so important
For everyone's self worth
And so we go out
To see, say
What's up
Black out what got you down
And was very loud and very gone.
And God's love language is silence. Makes sense of the distance

*

I CANT EVEN HEAR MY OWN VOICE
I CANT EVEN BREATHE MY OWN MIND
YET I CAN READ YOURS
I WONT EVER LEAVE YOU ON TIME
I MIGHT NOT LEAVE AT ALL
IM STILL CAUGHT UP IN RHYME
I STILL FEEL THE LEAVES FALL

JOSEPH MATICK

*

Someone replaced all of my meaning
With feeling

Without so much as a goodbye

If you see them, tell them
If you see me again and I am happy
Please remember

And remind me
It was you
Who knew so little of anything
To casually leave everything

Behind for me
My prayers are silent, deadly and direct.
My congregation is the washing machine
I leave for New York in a few days to do two or three
ambitious young man's dreams. The young man is
myself, I tell you.
They aren't mine and they are easier to achieve as a
result.
My dream is to lay here in hooch with her, waiting
for the call of justice
In the form of a kid's voice, two or three who are
mine. Ages 8 or 9.
Ready kids.
Fresh off the milked breast and determined to set old
men on fire.

GOOD LOOKING POMES

I—being their old man, will be spared. But not by them, by me.
I will think like a child, carry the imagination over seas and c-sectioned orphans and immigration papers drawn and quartered.
Stamped and dismembered.
I am a member of society
A nose up notoriety
An object of sobriety
I am a prized horse cutting tape with curious nostrils.
I have kicked off the jockey.
The little Italian man now makes middle eastern hooch.
I have watched every TV televangelist politician drown themselves on mass suicide in navy blue suits and red ties with blue notions of surrender.
All complicit and explicit the war ends in past tense passing tents and carpets cut
And no umbilical
I am a miracle and I am wearing Hermès spring summer for walking on sacred churches back home.

*

You have a beautiful mouth if you are here and you are today and in the future when you are perhaps not, everyday, all the time.
To use your mouth appropriately, use your heart.
To use your heart, know that it is okay even when it is not
It is often not.
But tonight may all things be okay.

JOSEPH MATICK

And okay not seem dismissive
My friend is texting me and my fingers are moving
fast and everyone knows how it feels to be delusional
and until you are called some distinguished
something
I, on the one hand, extinguish all devils and thoughts
at once
On the other hand,
I write
I mean with
With my hand I die in the arms of your affection
Blacking a page endlessly, my canvas
My coffin
Entirely mobile, and shaped expansively and never
ending
As earth
After all I will live and die here
And I will not die
Until I have loved
I mean lived
I mean to do both
I meant, I both'd, I conquered
Nothing if not this moment
Finally
Thank you for listening
Even if you aren't
Even if you're far away thinking about your reading
Or me
Writing what you are reading.

I.

I, I think
I drift, I drink, I drown
I think, I smile, I nod
I nod, I smile, I think, I read
I think to say something clever, and permanent and forever
I think to speak in French then in English
I fight the lost cause
I carry the losing man's torch to prove something
Can you hear it can you feel it
Will you be just like me for a moment
All the old men and young men are dead
Do not despair
When you bury me I'll be looking up and laughing at the cement
And how damning I took everything so small
Life is small
Unless
If you think about life being big it gives you the same relief as my last statement, you should say it is big
Very big and very grand

I am allowed to change my mind, my life, my phrasing
I am allowed to pray, to perish, to practice, to pretend to be immovable.
It is only in the speaking of words and perfect liturgical words that pretending tends to prophecy
I tend therefore I am
And I am a gardener
I am a fervent supporter of the universal heart
And it's nemesis for I cannot be me without context
Without friction
To err is Shakespearean and dumb and categorical and scholastic
Where are my friends
Got a billion in me

JOSEPH MATICK

I am not I
Said the fly
I can now fly
Said all pigs
In all nations
In all dialects
In all eras and tongues
And in every darkest part of your brain
May you find light
Tonight is beautiful
That's it.

*

Sometimes when I am I, I am asked to read and tonight and to breathe while pressing my lips together and make phonetic sounds that are perfectly understood and wholly unclear to the brain
Wholly relevant to the heart

JOSEPH MATICK

I will expire and believe in the vibration and the distance from my tongue to your eternal physical parts and all parts non-physical until you stop thinking about me or you or listening or being or not being or receiving or understanding or if not understanding is a force greater than your heart.
It is not.
Your heart beats
My God beats and beats me up and is a bad and negligent father or something.
These are all words
If I knew what they meant I would read poetry
And tonight and forever

I would cross out my eyes and hope to die in the
loving arms of a great big joke
One that laughs and lasts forever and says "you took
going away too seriously" and not a moment too fast
you awake in the eyes of a mother
On a stiff chair or a leather couch or being embraced
by an ottman and they all kiss you as clouds rain
epiphanies on a newborn baby.
I'm only thirty-five or something
I hope I mean something to you
I hope you never think of me as a self or anything
And you see me in you enough to not laugh at a
beating heart and you can live long
With big blood and long ventures
Down the veins and ventricles of your arms
Extending out and kissing all the parts left
untouched

JOSEPH MATICK

I came, I saw, I acclimated
I was unsatisfied
I came back
You can be me now
You can be anyone
Anyone else

GOOD LOOKING POMES

If you cross the street, just know there are so many streets and they all split directions and anyway they are man-made structures meant to think you are meant to move anywhere
You are immovable you are light
Goodnight

JOSEPH MATICK

*

I used to go to the cemetery, to write, to return and become at ease—
I lived next to Forest Lawn in Toluca Lake.
None of the tombstones are legible unless you get intimate with the ground.

I looked for Arthur Lee's grave.
I never found it.
I stopped looking.
And one day, leaving the cemetery, navel gazing
I read the words "Love."

There lies love
Still does

GOOD LOOKING POMES

Love lies?
No.
But it does die.
That line and the time I died
Are the only times I lied.

Keep this safe.

JOSEPH MATICK

About the Author

Joseph Matick is an American poet living in Paris.

This writing is courtesy of Avec Jack and Vera Pr also known as AJV and in collaboration with and in defiance of your local government.

ALSO OUT ON FAR WEST

SONNY VINCENT	Snake Pit Therapy
BRENT L. SMITH	Pipe Dreams on Pico
JOSEPH MATICK	The Baba Books
KURT EISENLOHR	Stab the Remote
KANSAS BOWLING	A Cuddly Toys Companion
KANSAS BOWLING & PARKER LOVE BOWLING	Prewritten Letters for Your Convenience
CRAIG DYER	Heavier Than a Death in the Family
PARKER LOVE BOWLING	Rhododendron, Rhododendron
JENNIFER ROBIN	You Only Bend Once with a Spoonful of Mercury
JOSEPH MATICK	Cherry Wagon
RICHARD CABUT	Disorderly Magic
NORMAN DOUGLAS	Love and the Fear of Love
ELIZABETH ELLEN	Estranged
JEFFREY WENGROFSKY	The Wolfboy of Rego Park
HAKON ADALSTEINSSON	Our Broken Land
.A FAR WEST ANTHOLOGY	Pretty Obscure
LILY LADY	NDA
NIKOLA PEPERA	Lay Down & Get Lost
JACK SKELLEY	Myth Lab
PETER CROWLEY	Down at Max's
STEVE KRAKOW	A Mind Blown Is A Mind Shown
ADDISON FULTON	Social Animals
TONY O'NEILL	Forged Prescriptions
CYNTHIA ROSS	The Secret Door
ROBERT LUNDQUIST	MASS
RICHARD CABUT	Ripped Backsides
MIKE DONOVAN	List of Band Names
DANIELLE CHELOSKY	Female Loneliness Epidemic
JUSTIN P. HOPPER	Dead the Long Year

farwestpress.com
+1 (541) FAR-WEST

www.ingramcontent.com/pod-product-compliance
Lightning Source LLC
LaVergne TN
LVHW041627070526
838199LV00052B/3270